>> **CODE** POWER: **A TEEN PROGRAMMER'S GUIDE**™

GETTING TO KNOW

Python

SIMONE PAYMENT

rosen
central

NEW YORK

Published in 2015 by The Rosen Publishing Group, Inc.
29 East 21st Street, New York, NY 10010

Library of Congress Cataloging-in-Publication Data

Payment, Simone, author.
Getting to know Python/Simone Payment.—First edition.
pages cm.—(Code power: a teen programmer's guide)
Audience: Grades 5 to 8.
Includes bibliographical references and index.
ISBN 978-1-4777-7717-6 (library bound)—ISBN 978-1-4777-7719-0 (pbk.)—ISBN 978-1-4777-7720-6 (6-pack)
1. Python (Computer program language)—Juvenile literature. 2. Computer programming—Juvenile literature. I. Title.
QA76.73.P98P39 2015
005.13'3—dc23

2013046858

Manufactured in the United States of America

{CONTENTS

C omputer programs run cell phones, televisions, cars, traffic signals, elevators, and kitchen appliances. And, of course, they run computers. There are hundreds of thousands of computer programs in use around the world and many thousands of programmers writing them. Many of these programmers use Python to write their programs. Python is a simple programming language with many uses. Most programmers find it easy to learn and easy to use. This book provides an overview of the many advantages of the Python programming language.

Before deciding on a computer programming language to learn, it might be logical to ask, "Why learn to write computer programs?" One reason is that it can be a lot of fun. Programming does take some practice. However, it is not just professional computer programmers who write programs. Even beginners can make a computer do something cool using just a few lines of simple code. Once a programmer learns some general rules and builds up some experience, programming becomes easier. Then the fun can really begin. For example, even beginning

sidenav = false;

UCTION

>> With a laptop and some programming skills, anyone can design a website, create a game, or build a phone app.

programmers who are learning to program as a hobby can design a game for their computer or smartphone, or write a program to analyze baseball stats.

Learning to program is also practical: programmers can write a program that makes a computer or other device do something no one else has asked it to do. Programmers do not have to be stuck only doing things with a computer that some other programmer thought someone might want to do. This allows a programmer to design something original and personalize a program to suit his or her needs. A programmer could write a computer program to create a database of DVDs or model cars, for example. Or a programmer might design a website dedicated to a favorite singer.

Another reason to learn computer programming is to understand more about computers and how they "think." Although programming is based on rules, there is also a great deal of creativity involved in thinking like a computer and solving problems. Computer programmers often take a complex goal and break it down into smaller building blocks in order to reach that objective. Breaking down the goal requires clear thinking and good problem-solving skills.

Yet another reason learning to program is beneficial is that it can help people get a job. Nearly every profession uses computers. Therefore, programmers are relied on to adapt programs to a profession's particular needs. Many companies are looking for skilled, creative programmers who know how to write good code.

After deciding to learn to program, the next decision is what programming language to learn. People choose to use a particular programming language for many reasons. Some reasons are personal. For example, some programmers might want to learn a programming language quickly. Others might want to be challenged by a more difficult language. Some programmers choose a language based on what they want to program. Some programming languages are designed for specific purposes, such as web programming. Others are more flexible and have many uses.

Python is an excellent choice as a programmer's first language for many reasons. The main reasons are that Python is easy to learn, is simple to use, and is a multipurpose language. Python can be learned quickly, and there are plenty of books, websites (including the official Python site at http://python.org, which offers tutorials and modules, among other resources), and other Python users that can help new programmers get started.

CHAPTER 1

FIRST THINGS FIRST: COMPUTERS AND PROGRAMMING

Before learning about programming languages in general, or Python specifically, it's important to know a little about computers and how they work.

THE BASIC PARTS

Computers have both external and internal parts. External parts are accessories such as a keyboard, mouse, and monitor (or screen). Other external parts might include ports for power cords or printer cords. Computers also have data ports for thumb drives or other external storage devices.

Some of the external parts are known as "input" devices. These allow a user to give information to a computer. An example of an input device might be a mouse or keyboard. Other devices are "output" devices. These accessories allow the computer to provide information to the user. A screen or monitor is an example of an output device.

Internal parts include a hard drive and a processor. The hard drive is where data is stored. The computer has different types of memory. Some "memories" are used by the computer

>> Cell phones, laptops, and other computers have ports that allow users to plug in external devices to extract or store data.

when it is running but disappear when the computer shuts down. Other types of memories are stored in the hard drive. These types of memories can be accessed again and again by the processor.

The processor is the "brain" of the computer. It is usually called a CPU, which stands for central processing unit. The CPU stores and retrieves information from the memory in the hard drive. It also does math. The CPU's other job is to carry out the instructions given by a computer program.

>> It's not just computers that use binary code: Braille and Morse code also use a binary (on/off) system to convey information.

Although the CPU is known as the brain of the computer, it isn't necessarily smart. It is just a machine that responds to what is known as binary code. "Binary" means on or off, and all computer code is made up of strings of just two numbers: 1 and 0. To the computer, 1 means "on," and 0 means "off." The CPU is made up of electrical circuits that are either on or off. The 1s and 0s of computer code tell the circuits what to do—whether to turn on or off.

>> THE BASICS

Computer users were on their own in the early days of computers. There were no word processing programs, no graphics programs, no spreadsheets, and no web browsers. (In fact, the Internet did not yet exist.) There were not many computers in existence. Those who had access to them were usually scientists or researchers at universities or large companies. These users had to write their own programs in order for the computer to do any task. Many users programmed in a language called BASIC, which stands for Beginner's All-purpose Symbolic Instruction Code. Mathematicians at Dartmouth College created BASIC in 1964. Home computer users began using it in the 1970s. A modified form of BASIC is still in use today.

>> This UNIVAC 11 computer from 1962 was the first commercial computer made in the United States. In the background are rolls of magnetic tape on which data was stored.

COMMUNICATING WITH THE "BRAIN"

Humans obviously don't communicate easily in 1s and 0s. That's why computer programs are needed. They "translate" our human language into a language the computer can understand with its 1/0, on/off brain. Therefore, computers need computer programs in order to function and follow human commands.

Computer programs are a set of instructions to the computer. These instructions, also called commands or statements, are written line by line. For example, a simple command to a computer looks like this:

print ("Hello, World!")

This line of code tells the computer to print the words "Hello, World!" on the screen.

The commands are strung together into a group. As a group, these instructions are called a program. A single program, or a group of programs working together, is also known as software. The computer carries out each individual command in the program. Then it moves on to the next instruction in the program. For example, a program to make a computer do some simple math would look like this:

print "10 + 8 is", 10 + 8
print "5 * 5 is", 5 * 5

The computer will print the words and numbers that are in between the quotation marks, perform the calculation, and then move on to the next line and do the same steps in that line. When the program runs, the screen would look like this:

10 + 8 is 18
5 * 5 is 25

Computer programmers write instructions to a computer in a language the computer can understand. These programs can "teach" the computer to do tasks that might be difficult or time consuming for humans. For example, a program can instruct a computer to analyze a series of millions of numbers. For a human, that task could take days. It would also take a lot of brainpower. For a computer, once it has its instructions, the task is simple.

The instructions within a computer program have to be exactly right or the computer won't do what it is being asked to do. Details are very important. This is why programs can't be written in everyday human language (such as English). Human language isn't clear and specific enough for computers. For example, in many languages, some words have multiple meanings. Computers aren't able to figure out which definition of the word is meant. In addition, arranging the same words in a different order can mean something completely different. This could also confuse the computer.

A LITTLE ABOUT OPERATING SYSTEMS

An operating system (or "OS") is a type of computer software. Microsoft Windows, Linux, and OS X (Macintosh) are three major

>> Just as there are several different operating systems for computers, there are different operating systems for smartphones, called mobile operating systems (or "mobile OS"). This Apple iPhone runs on iOS.

operating systems. Smartphones also have an operating system, such as Android or iOS. An operating system is the only type of computer software that can "talk" directly to the two types of computer hardware: the processor and the hard drive. Other computer programs must "ask" the OS to do things that involve the processor or hard drive. This is so that programs don't have to be written in different ways for each type of computer or smartphone.

Some current programming languages, such as Python, Java, or Visual Basic, have an interface between the program and the hardware to run the program. The interface is called a virtual machine or interpreter. These are like translators that are go-betweens for the program and the operating system. An advantage of using an interpreter is that it is more secure. Another advantage is that it makes programs more flexible because they can run on a wide variety of machines. There are many interpreters available for Python. Some examples are Jython (used with Java), CPython (used with C), and IronPython (used with C#).

An interpreter or virtual machine also needs a shell that allows a user to interact with it. The virtual machine gets commands from the keyboard and follows the instructions. Then it shows the results on screen. A fancier version of this is called an integrated development environment (IDE). An IDE is a graphical user interface (GUI) that has windows and menus on-screen just like a browser or software like Microsoft Word.

WHY SO MANY LANGUAGES?

Humans communicate with each other in many different languages, such as English, Spanish, Chinese, Hindi, or Arabic.

Humans can also communicate with computers in many different languages. Different programming languages have developed for various reasons. Some were created to serve a specific purpose. For example, the JavaScript programming language came about to do Web programming. SQL was developed to program databases.

Other languages came about because a programmer was unhappy with how an existing program worked. Python is such a language. Its creator, Guido Van Rossum, was dissatisfied with the language he was using to do his job. He decided he could do better. Van Rossum developed Python in his spare time, over many years. He got lots of input from early users of the program. Python continues to change and grow with feedback from thousands of present-day users.

WHEN PROGRAMMING GOES WRONG: BUGS

Errors in a computer program are called bugs. There are three types of bugs: syntax, runtime, and semantic. Syntax bugs break the "rules" of the program. If there are syntax errors in a program, the program will not run at all. Runtime errors are less serious errors. A program with a runtime error might begin running but stop when the program comes across the problem. A semantic error will also allow the program to run. However, the program won't do what the programmer intended it to do.

Looking for and fixing bugs is called debugging. Debugging is an important part of programming. To debug, programmers must

>> THE FIRST BUG WAS ACTUALLY A MOTH

On September 9, 1947, a moth was found to be the reason why Harvard University's Mark II computer had stopped working. Engineers had used the term "bug" previously to describe problems with machinery. The computer operators at Harvard were amused to find an actual bug in their computer. They taped the moth into a logbook that they kept to track problems with the Mark II computer. Underneath the bug they wrote, "First actual case of bug being found."

look at clues to figure out what went wrong. The programmer comes up with an idea about the possible problem and tries to fix the error. If the programmer's guess was right, the program can be fixed and will run. If the initial guess was wrong, the programmer must come up with new possibilities for what went wrong and then make another attempt to fix the problem. This process continues until the problem is solved.

Debugging takes some practice. There are tips and techniques for debugging, but the process mostly just takes experience and practice—and sometimes a lucky guess. However, some programmers consider debugging part of the fun of programming.

PYTHON: THE BASICS

W ith a little background about computers and programming, it's time to find out more about the Python programming language.

SO WHAT *IS* PYTHON?

Python is a general-purpose, high-level, interpreted language. What all those terms mean might not be obvious to someone who does not yet know how to program. However, broken down into parts these terms become easier to understand.

"General purpose" simply means that Python can be used for almost any type of programming task. Unlike languages that were created to do only one or two specific jobs, Python can be used for a wide range of programming work. It can be used for web programming, game programming, and many other types of tasks.

"High-level" languages are those programming languages that don't talk directly to the computer. C, C++, Perl, and Java are other examples of high-level programming languages. Python, like other high-level languages, is too complicated for

>> Python is a useful language for game programming. Entire games can be created in Python, or Python can add features such as 3-D to existing game programs written in other languages.

the computer to understand. Computers can only understand low-level languages. Low-level languages are also called machine languages or assembly languages. For a high-level language to work on a computer, the computer must process the language first. Only after processing the language can the computer run the program. The drawback to this is that high-level languages take a little longer to run. This is because the computer must go through two steps—processing *and* running the program.

However, there are many advantages of high-level programming languages. One is that programs written in high-level languages are much easier for programmers to write. They are also shorter. Both of these things contribute to making it faster for a programmer to write code in these languages. Because they are shorter and simpler, usually there are fewer errors in programs written in a high-level language. When there are mistakes in a program, it is usually easier to find them because the code is short.

Yet another advantage of high-level languages is that they are portable. This means they can run on any type of computer. Low-level languages, on the other hand, are specific to a type of computer. To run a program written in a low-level language on another type of computer, a programmer would need to rewrite or modify the program for the different machine.

Finally, Python is called an interpreted language because for a program written in Python to "talk" in a low-level language, an interpreter is needed. The interpreter reads the high-level language (Python) and carries out its instructions.

>> PYTHON PROGRAMMER PROFILE: TOM RYAN

Tom Ryan is a senior technical director at Epsilon, a marketing services company in Wakefield, Massachusetts. Ryan has been programming for more than twenty-five years and first learned to program when he was seventeen. His father worked for computer maker IBM and was able to get the family an early IBM personal computer. Ryan first used the BASIC programming language "because it was pretty easy to learn." Also, the computer game he wanted to play was written in BASIC. Knowing BASIC allowed Ryan "to actually rewrite the code in the game" in his favor. When Ryan played, he "always won and when [his] brother played the same game, he always lost." Because Ryan's brother lost every time, it allowed him "to get more time on the PC."

Continuing his interest in computers, Ryan got a B.A. in computer science from the State University of New York at Potsdam and then an MBA from Babson College. Over his career in computer programming, Ryan has learned many programming languages, including BASIC, PASCAL, C, COBOL, RGP, FORTRAN, IBM 360 Assembler, Intel x86 Assembler, Oracle PL/SQL, SQL Server Cursors, SAS, VB, C#, Perl, Python, Java, JavaScript, and VBscript. He currently codes in Perl, Python, VB, Java, and JavaScript.

Ryan first learned Python on the job. "The developer who had originally written the code for many of [the company's] clients left the company about one year after I started." So Ryan became the programmer in charge of Python-based coding at Epsilon. To learn Python, Ryan used "Internet searches, online books and websites, physical books, and existing code within the company." His method for learning the language was partly based on learning from books and other resources, and partly based on "experimentation and testing." With his "computer science/programming background," Ryan was "able to pick it up pretty quickly." After he learned the basics of Python, he developed some new applications in the language for other uses at Epsilon.

Ryan currently uses Python for processing client files. Python is used for formatting and cleaning up data files from clients and compiling client reports. Python also interacts with their operating system (Windows) to generate reports for the programmers on system functions. They also use Python to do file cleanup and maintenance on the servers. Ryan and his coworkers use other programming languages as well; most often they use Perl.

One of Python's advantages is its "ability to pack a lot of functionality into the code," Ryan reports. Its flexibility is also an advantage.

(continued on page 22)

(continued from page 21)

Ryan says programmers "can do multiple functions with simple expressions." Some of Python's requirements can be disadvantages, however. For example, the use of indents to indicate blocks of code makes Python easy to read. But "if the indentations don't line up, the code doesn't work and can sometimes be a bear to debug." Also, a colon (":") is used after certain statements (if, for, while). Ryan says he still gets "caught on missing the ':' every once in a while."

Ryan has some great advice for beginning programmers. He says to "learn as much as you can and utilize the resources that exist beyond what you have in front of you. There are numerous examples online of how to write something or perform a function. Utilize user support groups and blogs." He advises that programmers should "keep in mind that there is usually more than one way to solve a problem when coding." In fact, someone once told Ryan, "There's only been one line of code ever written. Everyone else has just taken it and modified it to do what they needed it to do." Another bit of advice is that programmers should "always remember to account for the unexpected as that's usually what causes the code to fail." Perhaps most important, Ryan reminds programmers to "enjoy what you do and do what you enjoy."

PYTHON TOOLS

To run Python code, two things are needed: an editor and an interpreter. An editor saves the code the programmer is currently writing. There are a large number of editors that can be used by Python programmers. Just a few of the many editors are code-Editor, DreamPie, DrPython, and LeoEditor.

As discussed in the section about operating systems, an interpreter allows users to interact directly with the computer

>> Members of Monty Python's Flying Circus (*pictured left to right*) included John Cleese, Terry Gilliam, Terry Jones, Graham Chapman, Michael Palin, and Eric Idle. The British TV show ran from 1969 to 1974.

to test their code. An interpreter takes the commands the user inputs into the keyboard and then follows the instructions given in the program. The results of the program show up on-screen. IDLE is an example of a Python IDE. (The name "IDLE" is also a Python in-joke because Eric Idle was one of the members of *Monty Python's Flying Circus*, for which Python is named.) Other examples of Python IDEs are Wing 101, Komodo, Spyder, and MonkeyStudio.

Modules are another type of tool. They are a way of organizing code. Some have specific functions. For example, PyGame is a module programmers can use to write games. It is free and runs on any operating system. A standard library is a collection of modules available to programmers. One of Python's strongest points is that it has a large standard library. This means that users do not have to start from scratch each time they begin a new project. There may be modules available in the standard library that can be reused for many purposes.

CHAPTER 3

WHY USE PYTHON?

There are plenty of programming languages on the market. Some programming languages fill one specific need, while other languages have many uses. So why use Python?

IN THE PLUS COLUMN

Python has many advantages over other available computer programming languages. One big advantage is that it is free. Python is available for download on the Web, at no cost. Python has many tools that are also free. The tools are also easy to find on the Internet.

Another major advantage is that Python is easy to learn and simple to use. Most people can learn Python in a few days. People who already know how to program in another language might be able to learn Python in just a few hours.

Because Python is widely used by programmers, there has already been a lot written about it. There are books and Web tutorials that can help a new user learn Python quickly. These resources make it easy to get help in learning and mastering Python.

>> Conferences or informal meetings give programmers a chance to learn from each other and swap tips. On big projects, professional programmers often work on teams, so good teamwork skills are important.

Another advantage of the fact that Python is widely used by programmers is that it is also simple to find someone else using it. Experienced Python programmers can provide help with problems or teach beginners helpful tips and tricks. New Python users can find this type of help online. They can also get help in person at local Python user group meetings. Many user groups meet once a month. The gatherings are a way for Python programmers to swap tips and give other programmers ideas about new ways of using Python. In many locations around the world, there are annual Python conferences once a year or more frequently. These conferences—usually called PyCons—even have programs geared toward teaching Python to kids.

With so many people using Python, there are many existing programs written in Python. New users can look at programs that other people have written to get ideas about how to do their own programming in Python. There are also many "parts" that can be reused in new programs.

Another main benefit of using Python is that it is very easy to write. Code written in Python is a great deal shorter than other programming languages such as Java or C++. For example, a program written in C might have twenty lines, and in Java it would have seven. In Python, the code to accomplish the same task might be only one line long. This is an advantage because it means that programs take less time to write. Shorter programs also usually reduce the possibility of making mistakes. There is less code to update in the future if changes are needed at a later time.

Python code is easy to read because it doesn't use a lot of symbols like curly braces ({) that are found in other programming languages. This makes it easy for people to read and understand code written by someone else. For example, the simple command shown earlier to print "Hello, World!" in Python, looks like this:

```
print ("Hello, World!")
```

The same command in Java looks like this:

```
public class HelloWorld {
    public static void main (String[] args) {
        System.out.println("Hello, world!");
    }
}
```

>> The flexibility of Python is one of its major advantages. Python programmers don't need to learn a new language if they switch from a PC to a Mac or UNIX machine.

The fact that Python runs on any operating system is yet another advantage of the language. Macintosh, UNIX, and PC users alike can run their machines with Python.

Because Python is a general-purpose language, it has many applications. Programmers can do almost anything with Python code. Python is flexible and always changing. Its uses continue to grow as the language is updated and improved by Python creator Guido Van Rossum and other Python users.

Python can work well with programs written in other languages. This allows programmers who usually work in another language to use Python for tasks that their programming language can't handle. Python users can also use code that has been developed in another language and easily integrate it with their Python code.

Python runs immediately. There is no need to use a compiler, which is a type of computer program that converts code into another programming language. For example, the Java programming language uses a compiler to translate source code into a language a computer can understand. This is not necessary in Python, which makes it simpler and easier to use.

Another advantage of Python is that it has what is called an interactive shell. This allows users to test their programs to see if the program will run correctly. The interactive shell provides a quick check for programmers to make surethat they are on the right track.

Unlike with many other programming languages, if there are errors in Python code, the system does not always crash. Instead, Python creates a list of problems. This makes it easier to find errors and fix them quickly. The way Python is written also cuts down on errors because certain errors that normally can happen in computer programs do not occur in Python code.

IN THE MINUS COLUMN

The list of drawbacks to using Python is very short. No computer programming language can do everything anyone would want it to do. Python is no exception. Therefore, it may be necessary to learn more than one language to do specific tasks. For example, to program 3-D games, a user might want to learn Alice. For some Web programming tasks, a user might want to learn PHP or MySQL.

>> WHAT DOES IT TAKE TO BE A PROGRAMMER?

People who design computer programs for a living are called computer programmers, software engineers, or software developers. Being a computer programmer requires creativity and problem-solving skills, as well as the ability to learn and follow the rules of a language. Computer programmers use skills from math, engineering, and science. Math provides the "language" for, and ways of working with, numbers. Engineering supplies the knowledge of design of systems or processes. From science, computer programmers learn the ability to observe, form a hypothesis, and test the hypothesis (and then form a new hypothesis if necessary).

The good news is that people who already know one programming language find it easy to learn a second (or third or fourth) programming language.

USES FOR PYTHON

Because Python is a flexible language, it can be used for many different tasks. Python is used in system programming and database programming. It can be used in game development and to control robots. Graphical user interface (GUI) programming, the design of the screens and buttons that allow users to interact with computers and other devices, uses Python. Various types of numeric and scientific programming utilize Python.

>> Programmers at a wide range of top companies use Python to do their daily tasks. At YouTube, programmers have used Python since the start of the company.

Many companies are using Python to run their products or websites. For example, Google uses Python to power its search engine. YouTube uses Python on its website, too. Instagram. com, Pinterest.com, and Rdio.com all power their websites with Python.

SurveyMonkey, an online survey company, redeveloped its survey system in Python. Chuck Groom, head of engineering, says that Python made it easier for them to add new features to their website. The fact that it is so easy to learn Python also helped SurveyMonkey's new employees learn their jobs more quickly.

>> PYTHON ON THE BATTLEFIELD

One of the organizations that uses Python is the U.S. military. COMBATXXI is a war games modeling program that allows military officials to plan for various battle scenarios. COMBATXXI takes maps and other types of real-world information and uses Python to develop models of what might happen on the battlefield. Python's flexibility allows COMBATXXI users to update information as events happen. This allows military planners and troops to better react to changing conditions on the battlefield.

A company called ForecastWatch used Python to develop its software, which is utilized by weather forecasters. The ForecastWatch system takes weather data from all around the world and compares it to forecasts to check their accuracy. Eric Floehr, the creator of ForecastWatch, says Python's flexibility has helped them grow and adapt their software as needed. Python also allowed them to develop ForecastWatch in a short amount of time.

Industrial Light and Magic uses Python to create its animated movies. Python controls its production systems and links its computer systems together to automate its production process. Pixar is another company that uses Python in the creation of its animated movies. Side Effects Software upgraded

>> Python can be used to program and run robots, like this iRobot bomb disposal robot used by the Denver Police Department bomb squad unit.

its 3-D special-effects software package using Python. This software, called Houdini, helps movie studios add special effects to their movies.

NASA programs in Python, and iRobot uscs Python in its robotic devices. Many banks program in Python to track the financial markets. Scientists use Python to write programs that analyze and organize vast amounts of data. Python is also used in aircraft design, earthquake prediction, and course scheduling at universities.

A NEW LANGUAGE IS HATCHED

P ython owes its existence to one man: Guido Van Rossum. Van Rossum created Python in the late 1980s and continues to be very involved in the development of the language. Python grew out of Van Rossum's need for a better programming language to do his work. However, Python also owes its existence to the work of many other people. Van Rossum believed that Python would be a better language if many people were involved in its improvement. He welcomed feedback from users and his fellow programmers. Python users continue to offer suggestions for improvements and upgrades. These changes have allowed Python to adapt to changing needs and new ways of using computers.

THE EARLY YEARS OF PYTHON

Guido Van Rossum was born on January 31, 1956, in the Netherlands. He graduated from the University of Amsterdam in 1982 with a degree in mathematics and computer science. Van Rossum put his degree to work with a programming job at CWI,

>> Python creator Guido Van Rossum speaks frequently at Python conferences and events. He is pictured here giving the keynote address at the 2008 PyCon.

a national research institute for mathematics and computer science in Amsterdam, the Netherlands.

At CWI, Van Rossum and his coworkers were using a programming language called ABC. Although ABC met most of his needs, Van Rossum did find many aspects of ABC frustrating. He felt he and his coworkers would be much more productive with a better language. Van Rossum considered using another existing programming language but didn't feel that any would do exactly what he wanted. "Being youthful at the time," he told *Computerworld* magazine, "I figured I could design and implement a language 'almost, but not quite, entirely unlike' ABC, improving upon ABC's deficiencies."

Late in 1989, Van Rossum set to work creating his own new programming language in his spare time. By early 1990, he had a rough working version. Van Rossum released version 0.9.0 on February 20, 1991. In a blog post about the history of Python, Van Rossum says he "immediately [got] a lot of feedback and with this encouragement I kept a steady stream of releases coming for the next few years."

In addition to creating Python, Van Rossum had to find a name for this new programming language. Van Rossum was a fan of the British comedy series *Monty Python's Flying Circus*. At the time he was creating the language, he was reading the scripts for the show. He states in his oral history on Docs.python.org that he wanted a name for his programming language "that was short, unique, and slightly mysterious." "Python" came to mind. Van Rossum liked that the name Python was "also catchy, a bit edgy, and at the same time, it fit in the tradition of naming languages after famous people, like Pascal, Ada, and Eiffel."

>> ADA, A PROGRAM AND A PROGRAMMER

Some computer programs are named after famous historical figures. The U.S. military created the Ada programming language in 1979 and named it in honor of Lady Ada Lovelace. Although she lived in England in the first half of the nineteenth century—before the time of computers as we now know them—Ada Lovelace is considered the first computer programmer. Lovelace worked with Charles Babbage, who had made plans for a machine called the analytical engine. Lovelace designed a program that would be fed into the machine on punch cards and would provide instructions to the machine.

>> Lady Ada Lovelace studied science and mathematics as a young woman. She predicted many of the modern-day uses of computers long before the first computer was ever built.

GROWTH OF PYTHON

After the official release of the Python language, more and more people began to use it, and Van Rossum continued to work on the development of the language in his spare time. Users would suggest improvements, and Van Rossum implemented the ideas he thought were worthwhile. As a result, Python continued to change and grow, which attracted even more users. By March 1993, there was an official newsgroup (still in existence at https://groups.google.com/forum/#!forum/comp.lang.python) where people could share information about Python. They could also ask questions and make suggestions for further changes.

PYTHON BECOMES A BIT MORE "OFFICIAL"

In the early years of Python, Van Rossum was using it to do some of his work at CWI in Amsterdam. But he was also using other programs, and much of the work he did on improving Python occurred after his regular work hours. In October 1994, Van Rossum came to the United States as a guest researcher at the U.S. National Institute of Standards and Technology (NIST) in Gaithersburg, Maryland. A few months later, in April 1995, he was offered a job in Reston, Virginia, at the Corporation for National Research Initiatives (CNRI). Van Rossum decided to move to the United States to take the job. One of the reasons he chose to make this big move was that his work on developing Python would be an official part of his job.

>> The NIST main administration building pictured here is near Washington, D.C. NIST is part of the U.S. Department of Commerce and sponsors research in many areas of science.

At CNRI, Van Rossum continued to release new and improved versions of Python. More people were using it for more types of projects. Van Rossum admitted to *Computerworld* magazine that initially he had "a pretty narrow view of Python's niche, and a lot of what people were doing [with Python] was completely unexpected."

In addition to making improvements to the Python language, Van Rossum made sure that Python remained an open-source language. This allowed Python to be available to anyone, for free, and for whatever use programmers had for the language.

Starting in 2000, Van Rossum began working at a series of start-up companies. Python was always a big part of his work at those companies, and he continued to change and grow the language. In 2005, Van Rossum was hired to work at Google. The company allowed him to spend about half of his work hours on the development of Python. In 2013, Van Rossum began working at Dropbox, where he continues to spend about half of his work time improving the Python language.

>> GUIDO VAN ROSSUM: BDFL

People call Guido Van Rossum "Benevolent Dictator for Life," or "BDFL," because he is ultimately in charge of the language (the "dictator") and intends to continue to be ("for life"). But he is also open to the suggestions of other programmers (so he is "benevolent"). Van Rossum earned this title in 1995 at a meeting of Python developers in Virginia. Everyone at the meeting was given a funny title. Van Rossum's was "First Interim Benevolent Dictator for Life." The title stuck, and eventually the "First Interim" part of the title was dropped. Van Rossum told *Computerworld* magazine that he likes the title because it "totally matches the whimsical outlook I try to maintain on Python."

THE PYTHON PHILOSOPHY

Several circumstances influenced Van Rossum's philosophy for Python. First, because Van Rossum developed Python on his own in his spare time, he didn't have money or a lot of time to spend on the program. This resulted in Van Rossum developing some rules for himself—and for Python. One of the main rules, which he describes in a blog post about Python's design philosophy, is "borrow ideas from elsewhere wherever it makes sense." Van Rossum looked around at other programming languages and evaluated what was good and bad about each. When he saw aspects of a program that made good sense, he incorporated them into Python.

Another idea came from Albert Einstein, who called for things to be simplified as much as seems reasonable. Van Rossum did whatever he could to make Python easy to use and understand, and with the least possible fuss. But the program had to be complex enough to handle all the tasks he hoped to accomplish.

A third aspect of Van Rossum's design philosophy was to not spend too much time making Python perfect. Instead, Van Rossum planned to fix and upgrade Python as he went along. As he states, "Don't try for perfection because 'good enough' is often just that." This would also allow other Python users to contribute to the improvement and growth of Python. Users could make suggestions for changes and upgrades. The Python user community could contribute to making Python a better and more flexible and useful language.

Other aspects of Van Rossum's design philosophy were not related to his need to save time while developing Python. These aspects were things that he wanted from the program and were not based on the restrictions of time and money he faced. A main goal was for Python to be available for all computer platforms, not just one. Another goal was for Python to allow the computer—not the programmer—to do the work. Van Rossum also wanted Python to have several "levels" that would allow users to extend the language to make it do what each user wanted or needed Python to do.

Van Rossum's experience using the program ABC when he was developing Python also influenced what he wanted from Python. The ABC program had tried to be the perfect program, the *only* program someone would need to use. While this may have been a worthwhile goal, it made ABC a difficult program to learn and use. This limited ABC's use to a certain group of users who could understand and learn this difficult program. Van Rossum wanted Python to be the exact opposite: easy to learn and use, and a flexible program that users could modify for their own needs.

>> Van Rossum welcomes input from any Python user who has a suggestion for improvement. Other users add their input on the suggestion; if it is a good one, Python is updated.

Van Rossum was not afraid to allow Python users to be part of the development of Python. All of the aspects of Python's design philosophy combined to make Python a success. Van Rossum says in a blog post about Python's design philosophy that early users of the language "found that Python worked 'well enough' for their purposes" and they made suggestions for improvements. Many of their suggestions "involved substantial changes and reworking of core parts of the language. Even today, Python continues to evolve." As Van Rossum states in the same blog post about Python's design philosophy, "In many ways, the design philosophy I used when creating Python is probably one of the main reasons for its success."

HOW DOES PYTHON STACK UP?

With so many programming languages in use, it is reasonable to consider other languages. What makes one better than another? Which ones are best for which tasks? Which one should a new programmer use? What are the positives and drawbacks of other languages?

Many programmers know more than one language. Each programmer may have a definite preference for a particular language but may need to use a second (or sixth) to accomplish specific tasks. Guido Van Rossum, creator of Python, gave some advice to programmers about this topic in *Computerworld* magazine. "Learn more than one language," Van Rossum suggested. "It's amazing how eye-opening it can be to compare and contrast two languages."

The following sections contain information on some major programming languages. Not every available programming language is covered.

>> Programmers who want to test their skills against other developers can enter competitions, like this computer game contest for teenagers in Germany.

THE "C"S

There are a group of languages based on the C programming language, including C++, C#, and Objective C. C is one of the original programming languages. Today, it is used often in game programming. However, it is not an easy language to learn. It is more complicated than Python. Therefore, it is not the best choice for a beginning programmer.

>> GAME AND GRAPHICS PROGRAMMING

In addition to Python's PyGame, there are many programming languages people can use to program games and create animations. Scratch is a language that can create both games and animations. Blitz Basic and Unity 3D are two other game programming languages. Adobe's Flash is software that programmers can use to create animations. Alice and Greenfoot are 3-D programming languages. There are also several programming languages that have many other uses but can also be used to create games. These languages include C, C++, C#, and Java.

C++ is also used in game programming. In addition, C++ is also often used for large programming projects worked on by multiple people at the same time. Like C, C++ is a little more complicated and challenging to learn than Python.

Another offshoot of C is C#. C# is similar to Java but is only for the Windows operating system. It is a little easier to learn than C or C++.

Objective C is similar to C. It is used on Apple computers, iPhones, and iPads. It is a fairly popular language. Many employers are looking for programmers who know Objective C.

JAVA

Java is a popular programming language often used for web applications and computer networking. It has many other uses as well. For example, it is used on Android phones. Like

Python, it is cross-platform, which means it can run on any operating system.

Java is a little more complicated than Python. However, there is a lot of information in books and Web sites about learning and using Java. It shares some features with C++, so programmers who already know C++ usually find it easy to learn Java. Many programming jobs require knowledge of Java. People who want to get a job as a programmer may want to consider learning Java.

JAVASCRIPT

Although it is similar to Java, JavaScript is a bit easier to learn. It is used for web programming and for creating games.

PHP

Another language often used in designing and building websites is PHP. PHP has other uses as well and is a popular language. Because there are many PHP users, it is easy to find help learning the language.

PERL

Perl is another language used for web development. It can be used on all operating systems. Perl is also used for database programming. Perl is a more complicated language than Python and is therefore more difficult to learn.

RUBY

Used mainly for web development, Ruby is a free program. It runs on all operating systems. Like Python, Ruby is easy to learn and is easy to read and write.

SCRATCH

Scratch is a fun programming language for creating animations, games, and stories. It is easy to learn and use. There is a lot of online support for Scratch users and places to post and share games and animations programmed in Scratch. Another advantage of Scratch is that it is free.

>> PYTHON PROGRAMMER PROFILE: DAVID YOUNG

Python user David Young is the chief technical officer (CTO) and cofounder of Blue Shell Games, a leading social casino games developer based in San Francisco, California. Before cofounding Blue Shell, he was the vice president of engineering at Slide, a consumer Internet startup acquired by Google in 2010.

Young began programming when he was just ten years old. He used the ANSI C language on an Apple IIgs computer. He attended a computer science program at the University of San Francisco but decided to pursue a major in English literature instead. Although he learned some programming during his time at the University of San Francisco, for the most part he taught himself to program.

Young and his coworkers at Blue Shell use Python to program games and to power the server for their social and mobile games. They chose Python because it "strikes a great balance between speed of development and quality of developed code." Young also uses Python because he says it is "a great language for quick one-off tasks that need to get done," such as data processing and manipulation.

Some companies choose languages that are a bit more formal and structured in an attempt to prevent any programmer errors. But, for a company like Blue Shell, which is a consumer Internet-focused

(continued on page 50)

(continued from page 49)

start-up, getting a product out to consumers as fast as possible is a high priority. Because Python is so easy to use, it makes it quick to write code and it is a good option for a company like Young's. Young also likes the fact that Python uses clean, straightforward language that avoids some of the complications that can come up with other languages. He concludes, "The end result is some pretty decent code that doesn't take too much time to write, which we're pretty happy with."

Young's team at Blue Shell also uses some of the tools available for Python, such as the gevent networking library and MongoDB and Redis databases "to build new features for our players quickly while maintaining great performance and reliable uptimes." Young says that Python "has a rich standard library and a great open-source ecosystem." Another advantage of Python is that users "have been contributing to Python's developer for almost 20 years now, so the language and libraries are generally mature and trustworthy."

Of course Python does have some weaknesses. One that Young has noticed is that although Python allows for customization (which is a good thing), Python's flexibility can also be a drawback. He says that you can make all kinds of creative changes when writing code in Python. However, when looking back at code written previously, it is "easy to forget what magic tricks you employed a year or five ago, although this is somewhat true in nearly every programming language. Python's flexibility can [make] this problem [worse]." Another weakness is that Python's "execution speed isn't the greatest, although it's much faster generally than some other languages." Young also points out that the differences between version 2.X and version 3.X of Python can be a little "intimidating" for beginners.

In addition to Python, Young and Blue Shell use "lots" of other languages. He says that a "modern technology business typically uses at least a scripting language, a client-side language, and a server-side language." At Blue Shell they also use "JavaScript (Browser), JavaScript (Node), Objective-C, Java (Android), and ActionScript."

Young has some good advice for beginning programmers: "It's widely held that true mastery of a task takes 10,000 hours, and it's especially true for programming. Never be afraid to try new ideas, new languages, tools, and remember to practice, practice, practice." Young adds that because "technology changes at such a rapid pace," for trained and untrained programmers alike "a programmer's education continues forever."

OTHER LANGUAGES TO CONSIDER

Programmers interested in coding for robotics should look into Arduino and Lego Mindstorms. Good languages for creating apps for smartphones and tablets are AppInventor and Codea. For web programming, Code Avengers and Thimble are two languages to try.

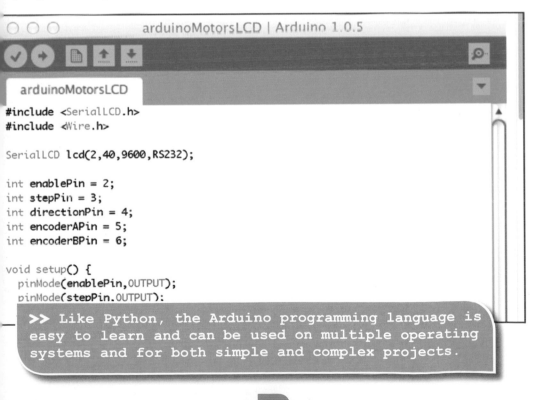

```
arduinoMotorsLCD | Arduino 1.0.5

arduinoMotorsLCD

#include <SerialLCD.h>
#include <Wire.h>

SerialLCD lcd(2,40,9600,RS232);

int enablePin = 2;
int stepPin = 3;
int directionPin = 4;
int encoderAPin = 5;
int encoderBPin = 6;

void setup() {
  pinMode(enablePin,OUTPUT);
  pinMode(stepPin,OUTPUT);
```

>> Like Python, the Arduino programming language is easy to learn and can be used on multiple operating systems and for both simple and complex projects.

Although there are many worthy programming languages on the market, the ease, simplicity, popularity, and flexibility of Python make it an ideal choice for beginning programmers. The success and popularity of Python surprises even Guido Van Rossum, Python creator. He told *Computerworld* magazine, "I certainly never expected anything of the sort when I got started." But Van Rossum is pleased with Python's many uses and successes. For Van Rossum, perhaps the most important legacy of Python is that "it has brought fun back to programming."

ACCESSORY An add-on that enhances the effectiveness of another object.

ANIMATION A moving cartoon or other type of artwork.

APPLICATION Putting an existing item to a new use; software or a computer program that performs a particular task.

BA Bachelor of arts, an education degree from a four-year college.

BRAILLE A writing system used by people who are sight-impaired. Letters are represented by a series of raised dots arranged in patterns.

DATABASE A collection of information organized in various ways.

ECOSYSTEM A complex community acting together.

HYPOTHESIS A tentative assumption to be tested.

INSTITUTE An educational organization, usually focused on a technical field.

INTERFACE A device or program enabling a user to communicate with a computer.

KEYNOTE A speech usually given at the beginning of a conference or meeting.

LEGACY Something transmitted from an older generation to a younger one.

MBA Master of business administration, a graduate degree.

MODULE A standardized unit for use together with others to create a program or to perform another function.

MORSE CODE An alphabet or code in which letters are represented by combinations of long and short signals of light or sound.

OBJECTIVE A goal or end product.

PHILOSOPHY A system of beliefs or guiding principles.

PLATFORM The computer equipment using a particular operating system.

PORT An interface at which a computer connects to another device.

PUNCH CARD A card with holes in it in specific positions to represent data.

SCENARIO A possible sequence of events.

SEMANTIC Of or relating to meaning in language.

SERVER A computer in a network that provides a service (such as data storage) to other computers in the network.

SPREADSHEET An accounting program for a computer; a document arranged with cells in a grid that is used to calculate data or organize information.

SYNTAX The way words are ordered to create meaning.

Canada's Association of IT Professionals (CIPS)
5090 Explorer Drive, Suite 801
Mississauga, ON L4W 4T9
Canada
Website: http://www.cips.ca
The CIPS works on behalf of information technology (IT) work-
ers and helps educate high school students about career
opportunities in IT.

Girls Who Code
28 West 23rd Street, 4th Floor
New York, NY 10010
Website: http://www.girlswhocode.com
The mission of Girls Who Code is to interest young women in
computer programming as a career and to give them skills
and resources to succeed in the field.

IEEE Computer Society
2001 L Street NW, Suite 700
Washington, DC 20036-4928
(800) 272-6657
Website: http://www.computer.org
The IEEE Computer Society is a good source of information on
various aspects of technology. It offers student member-
ships and sponsors conferences and other learning
opportunities.

Khan Academy
P.O. Box 1630
Mountain View, CA 94042
Website: https://www.khanacademy.org/cs/programming
Khan Academy is a nonprofit educational organization that
provides free course information on programming and other
topics.

Learning Labs
483 Queen Street West, 3rd floor
Toronto, ON M5V 2A7
Canada
Website: http://learninglabs.org
Learning Labs is an organization that helps programmers of all
ages learn new skills. Its programs Girls Learning Code and
Kids Learning Code are geared toward kids.

National Association of Programmers (NAP)
P.O. Box 529
Prairieville, LA 70769
Website: http://napusa.org
The NAP is a national group promoting the work of program-
mers. It offers resources to both professionals and students
in the field and sponsors various events.

Opensource.com
Red Hat, Inc.
100 East Davie Street
Raleigh, NC 27601

(919) 754-3700

Website: http://opensource.com

Opensource.com is dedicated to promoting open-source software use in business, education, government, health, law,
and life. It also offers information and resources for beginning coders.

Python Software Foundation (PSF)

9450 SW Gemini Drive

ECM# 90772

Beaverton, OR 97008

Website: http://www.python.org/psf

The PSF works to promote and develop the Python programming language and to support Python programmers around
the world.

WEBSITES

Due to the changing nature of Internet links, Rosen Publishing
has developed an online list of websites related to the subject of
this book. This site is updated regularly. Please use this link to
access the list:

http://www.rosenlinks.com/CODE/Python

Barry, Paul, and David Griffiths. *Head First Programming: A Learner's Guide to Programming Using the Python Language.* Sebastopol, CA: O'Reilly, 2009.

Briggs, Jason R. *Python for Kids: A Playful Introduction to Programming.* San Francisco, CA: No Starch Press, 2013.

Campbell, Jennifer, Paul Gries, Jason Montojo, and Greg Wilson. *Practical Programming: An Introduction to Computer Science Using Python.* Raleigh, NC: The Pragmatic Bookshelf, 2009.

Dawson, Michael. *Python Programming for the Absolute Beginner.* 3rd ed. Boston, MA: Course Technology, 2010.

Downey, Allen B. *Python for Software Design: How to Think Like a Computer Scientist.* New York, NY: Cambridge University Press, 2009.

Farrell, Mary E. *Computer Programming for Teens.* Boston, MA: Thomson Course Technology, 2008.

Goldsmith, Mike, and Tom Jackson. *Eyewitness Computer.* New York, NY: DK Publishing, 2011.

Harbour, Jonathan S. *Video Game Programming for Kids.* Boston, MA: Course Technology, 2013.

Harrison, Matt. *Treading on Python, Volume 1: Foundations of Python.* Seattle, WA: CreateSpace, 2012.

Harrison, Matt. *Treading on Python, Volume 2: Intermediate Python.* Seattle, WA: CreateSpace, 2013.

Jackson, Cari. *Revolution in Computers.* Tarrytown, NY: Marshall Cavendish Benchmark, 2010.

LEAD Project. *Super Scratch Programming Adventure! Learn to Program by Making Cool Games.* San Francisco, CA: No Starch Press, 2012.

Lutz, Mark. *Programming Python*. 4th ed. Sebastopol, CA: O'Reilly Media, Inc., 2009.

Monk, Simon. *Programming the Raspberry Pi: Getting Started with Python*. New York, NY: McGraw-Hill, 2013.

Otfinoski, Steven. *Computers*. Tarrytown, NY: Marshall Cavendish Benchmark, 2008.

Raum, Elizabeth. *The History of the Computer*. Chicago, IL: Heinemann Library, 2008.

Richardson, Matt, and Shawn Wallace. *Getting Started with Raspberry Pi*. Sebastopol, CA: Maker Media, 2013.

Rushkoff, Douglas. *Program or Be Programmed: Ten Commands for a Digital Age*. New York, NY: OR Books, 2010.

Sande, Warren, and Carter Sande. *Hello World! Computer Programming for Kids and Other Beginners*. 2nd ed. Greenwich, CT: Manning Publications, 2013.

Sweigart, Al. *Making Games with Python and Pygame: A Guide to Programming with Graphics, Animation, and Sound*. Seattle, WA: CreateSpace, 2012.

{BIBLIOGRAPHY

Barry, Paul, and David Griffiths. *Head First Programming*. Sebastopol, CA: O'Reilly, 2009.

Briggs, Jason R. *Python for Kids: A Playful Introduction to Programming*. San Francisco, CA: No Starch Press, 2013.

Campbell, Jennifer, Paul Gries, Jason Montojo, and Greg Wilson. *Practical Programming: An Introduction to Computer Science Using Python*. Raleigh, NC: The Pragmatic Bookshelf, 2009.

Downey, Allen B. *Python for Software Design: How to Think Like a Computer Scientist*. New York, NY: Cambridge University Press, 2009.

Goldsmith, Mike, and Tom Jackson. *Eyewitness Computer*. New York, NY: DK Publishing, 2011.

Hamilton, Naomi. "The A–Z of Programming Languages: Python." *Computerworld*, August 5, 2008. Retrieved November 2013 (http://www.techworld.com.au/article/255835/a-z_programming_languages_python/?, accessed August 9, 2013).

Lee, Kent D. *Python Programming Fundamentals*. London, England: Springer, 2011.

Lutz, Mark. *Learning Python*. 4th ed. Sebastopol, CA: O'Reilly, 2009.

Monk, Simon. *Programming the Raspberry Pi: Getting Started with Python*. New York, NY: McGraw-Hill, 2013.

Python Software Foundation. "Python: A Programming Language Changes the World." 2013. Retrieved November 2013 (http://brochure.getpython.info/, accessed October 2, 2013).

Pyvideo.org. "How and Why Python Is Being Used by the Military to Model Real-World Battlefield Scenarios." January 29, 2013. Retrieved November 2013 (http://pyvideo.org/video/318/pycon-2010--how-and-why-python-is-being-used-to-b, accessed September 30, 2013).

Sande, Warren, and Carter Sande. *Hello World! Computer Programming for Kids and Other Beginners*. Greenwich, CT: Manning Publications, 2009.

Summerfield, Mark. *Programming in Python 3: A Complete Introduction to the Python Language*. Upper Saddle River, NJ: Addison-Wesley, 2009.

Technica, Ars. "Dennis Ritchie, Father of C and Co-Developer of Unix, Dies." *Wired*, October 13, 2011. Retrieved September 26, 2013 (http://www.wired.com/wiredenterprise/2011/10/dennis-ritchie).

Van Rossum, Guido. "Personal History, Part 1, CWI." January 20, 2009. Retrieved August 9, 2013 (http://python-history.blogspot.com/2009/01/personal-history-part-1-cwi.html).

Van Rossum, Guido. "Personal History, Part 2, CNRI and beyond." January 27, 2009. Retrieved August 9, 2013 (http://python-history.blogspot.com/2009/01/personal-history-part-2-cnri-and-beyond.html).

Van Rossum, Guido. "Python's Design Philosophy." January 13, 2009. Retrieved August 9, 2013 (http://python-history.blogspot.com/2009/01/pythons-design-philosophy.html).

{ INDEX

ABOUT THE AUTHOR

Simone Payment has a degree in psychology from Cornell University and a master's degree in elementary education from Wheelock College. She is the author of twenty-nine books for young adults. Her previous book about Navy SEALs, *Inside Special Operations: Navy SEALs* (also from Rosen Publishing), won a 2004 Quick Picks for Reluctant Young Readers award from the American Library Association and is on the Nonfiction Honor List of Voice of Youth Advocates.

PHOTO CREDITS

Cover RapidEye/Vetta/Getty Images; p. 5 Netfalls/Remy Musser/Shutterstock.com; p. 9 Peter Gudella/Shutterstock.com; p. 10 ThomasLENNE/Shutterstock.com; p. 11 Earl Scott/Photo Researchers/Getty Images; p. 14 Canadapanda/Shutterstock.com; p. 19 Razmarinka/Shutterstock.com; p. 23 Everett Collection; p. 26 Bloomberg/Getty Images; p. 28 MacFormat Magazine/Future/Getty Images; p. 31 CTK/AP Images; p. 33 Andy Cross/The Denver Post/Getty Images; p. 35 Sauria Associates, LLC/Flickr Vision/Getty Images; p. 37 Science & Society Picture Library/Getty Images; p. 39 © Robert Rathe; pp. 42–43 © iStockphoto.com/vm; p. 46 Ulrich Baumgarten/Getty Images; p. 51 Used with permission of Arduino; cover and interior design elements © iStockphoto.com/letoakin (programming language), © iStockphoto.com/AF-studio (binary pattern), © iStockphoto.com/piccerella (crosshatch pattern).

Designer: Nicole Russo; Editor: Shalini Saxena;
Photo Researcher: Marty Levick